COMMON CORE CLINICS

Grade 8

CLINICS

English Language Arts

Reading Literature

Common Core Clinics, English Language Arts, Reading Literature, Grade 8
OT270 / 382NA

ISBN-13: 978-0-7836-8485-7

Cover Image: © fStop/Alamy

Triumph Learning® 136 Madison Avenue, 7th Floor, New York, NY 10016

© 2012 Triumph Learning, LLC
Coach is an imprint of Triumph Learning®

ALL ABOUT YOUR BOOK

COMMON CORE CLINICS will help you master important reading skills.

Each lesson has a **Learn About It** box that teaches the idea. A sample passage focuses on the skill. A **graphic organizer** shows you a reading strategy.

Each lesson has a **Try It** passage with **guided reading**.

 Higher-Order Thinking Skills

Questions that make you think further about what you read.

Apply It provides **independent practice** for reading passages, answering short-answer questions, and responding to writing prompts.

Table of Contents

Dialogue and Incidents

Learn About It

Dialogue refers to the words spoken between characters in a story. In fiction, dialogue is enclosed in quotation marks. In drama, dialogue comes directly after the name of the character who speaks. Dialogue has many purposes. It can establish the setting or mood of a story, reveal details about characters, or move the plot forward. Authors often use dialogue to create a closer connection between the reader and the characters.

Read the drama. As you read, try to figure out what the dialogue reveals about the background, plot, and characters of the story.

Setting: Walter and his sister Donna are in a ski resort. Walter has a cast on his right wrist.

WALTER: Do you think Mom will notice?

DONNA: Walter, your wrist is *broken*! What were you thinking, anyhow? Didn't you learn your lesson the last time you tried to ski that course?

WALTER: I *had* to! Nick *dared* me!

DONNA: Well, it's Dad you should be worried about. He's the only person who's ever skied down the Triple Diamond without wiping out. He's going to be furious!

WALTER: Do you think long sleeves will hide it?

What Dialogue Tells You		
Background Walter broke his wrist trying to ski a difficult course, something he has tried once before. His father is the only person who has ever conquered the course.	**Plot** Walter's parents are coming home soon, and he is going to try to hide his injury.	**Characters** Walter: reckless and daring Donna: protective Dad: expert skier

Try It

Read the passage. As you read, circle the dialogue that reveals information about the characters and how it helps establish the plot of the story. Use the questions to help you.

excerpted and adapted from

Dracula's Guest
by Bram Stoker

When we started for our drive, the sun was shining brightly on Munich, and the air was full of the joyousness of early summer. Just as we were about to depart, Mr. Delbruck (the owner of the Four Seasons Hotel, where I was staying) came down to the carriage and, after wishing me a pleasant drive, said to the coachman, "Remember to be back by nightfall. The sky looks bright, but there is a shiver in the north wind that says there may be a sudden storm. But I am sure you will not be late." Here he smiled and added, "For you know what night it is."

Johann answered with an emphatic, "Yes, sir," and, touching his hat, drove off quickly. When we had cleared the town, I said, after asking to him to stop:

"Tell me, Johann, what is tonight?"

He answered quickly, "Witches' Night," and started off rapidly, as if to make up for lost time. Every now and then the horses seemed to throw up their heads and sniff the air suspiciously. On such occasions I often looked round in alarm. The road on which we rode was pretty bleak, but as we drove, I saw a road that led through a little winding valley. It looked so inviting that, even at the risk of offending him, I called Johann to stop, and descended from the carriage to get a better look.

"Tell me," I said, "about this place where that road leads," and I pointed down.

He grew visibly nervous and mumbled a prayer before he answered, "It is cursed."

"What is cursed?" I enquired.

"The village."

"Then there is a village?"

"No, no. No one has lived there for hundreds of years."

His evasiveness only heightened my curiosity.

> The story opens with a cheerful scene. How does the dialogue change the mood of the story?

> What background information does this dialogue provide?

Continued on the next page ➡

Continued from the previous page

"But you said there was a village."

"There *was*."

"Where is it now?" I demanded.

Whereupon he burst out into a long story in German and English, so mixed up that I could not quite understand exactly what he said. He was evidently afraid to speak the last words. As he proceeded with his narration, he grew more and more excited. It seemed as if his imagination had got hold of him, and he ended almost paralyzed by fear—white-faced, perspiring, trembling, and looking around him as if expecting that some dreadful presence would set upon us there in the bright sunshine on the open plain.

> What kind of character is the narrator?

Finally, in an agony of desperation, he cried, "Witches' Night!" and pointed to the carriage for me to get in.

Standing back, I said, "You are afraid, Johann—you are afraid. Go home. I shall return alone; the walk will do me good." The carriage door was open. I took from the seat my oak walking stick—which I always carry on my holiday excursions—and closed the door, pointing back to Munich, and said, "Go home, Johann—Witches' Night doesn't concern Englishmen."

After giving the direction, "Home!," I turned to go down the cross road into the valley.

HOTS Analyze

Why do you think the narrator does not sympathize with Johann's fear?

Apply It

Read the drama. As you read, identify how the dialogue helps establish the background, plot, and characters of the story. Answer the questions that follow.

excerpted and adapted from

A Doll's House
by Henrik Ibsen

The setting is the house of Torvald and Nora Helmer. Enter NORA, humming a tune and in high spirits. She carries a number of parcels, which she lays on a table.

TORVALD: (*calls out from his room*) Is that my little hummingbird singing out there?

NORA: (*busy opening some of the parcels*) Yes, it is!

TORVALD: Is it my little squirrel bustling about?

NORA: Yes!

TORVALD: When did my squirrel come home?

NORA: Just now. Come in here, Torvald, and see what I have bought.

TORVALD: Don't disturb me. (*A little later, he opens the door and looks into the room, pen in hand.*) Bought, did you say? All these things? Has my little spendthrift been wasting money again?

NORA: Yes, but, Torvald, this year we really can let ourselves go a little. This is the first Christmas that we have not needed to economize.

TORVALD: Still, you know, we can't spend money recklessly.

NORA: Yes, Torvald, we may be a wee bit more reckless now, mayn't we? Just a tiny wee bit! You are going to have a big salary and earn lots and lots of money.

TORVALD: Yes, after the New Year; but then it will be a whole quarter before the salary is due.

NORA: We can borrow until then.

TORVALD: Nora! (*goes up to her and takes her playfully by the ear*) The same little featherhead! Suppose, now, that I borrowed fifty pounds today, and you spent it all in the Christmas week, and then on New Year's Eve a stone fell on my head and killed me, and—

NORA: (*putting her hands over his mouth*) Oh! Don't say such horrid things.

TORVALD: Still, suppose that happened. What then?

Continued on the next page ➤

Continued from the previous page

NORA: If that were to happen, I don't suppose I should care whether I owed money or not.

TORVALD: Yes, but what about the people who had lent it?

NORA: They? Who would bother about them? I should not know who they were.

TORVALD: Seriously, Nora, you know what I think about that. No debt, no borrowing. There can be no freedom or beauty about a home life that depends on borrowing and debt.

NORA: It's a shame to say that. I do really save all I can.

TORVALD: (*laughing*) That's very true, all you can.

NORA: (*smiling quietly and happily*) You haven't any idea how many expenses we skylarks and squirrels have, Torvald.

TORVALD: You are an odd little soul. Very like your father. You always find some new way of getting money, and, as soon as you have got it, it seems to melt in your hands.

NORA: Ah, I wish I had inherited many of Papa's qualities.

TORVALD: And I would not wish you to be anything but just what you are, my sweet little skylark.

Answer these questions about "A Doll's House." Write your answers in complete sentences.

1. What sort of language does Torvald use when addressing Nora?

_____

_____

2. What does the dialogue tell you about the nature of Torvald and Nora's relationship?

_____

_____

3. Based on their conversation, what can you conclude about Torvald and Nora's financial status?

_____

_____

4. How has their financial status changed recently?

_____

_____

5. How do Nora and Torvald differ in their approach to spending money?

_____

_____

6. Based on this dialogue, what are Torvald and Nora's main character traits?

_____

_____

Supporting an Analysis of Text

Learn About It

In order to properly **analyze** a work of fiction, you need to provide **evidence** from the text to support that analysis. Evidence can come in the form of specific lines or literary devices used in a poem, or in the form of dialogue, characterizations, and plot details in a story or drama.

Read the passage. As you read, pay attention to details that might support an analysis of the passage.

The duke's eyes blazed with a fiery envy as he slammed the door of his chamber behind him. "Upstaged by the prince once again!" he thought. "Made to look like a fool in front of those spineless courtiers! Bah! I'll be revenged upon him—I swear it!" Fuming, the duke took up his quill and began his scheming.

Evidence from Text	Analysis
"blazed with a fiery envy" Angry that he has been embarrassed in public Seeks revenge Looks down on others Begins "scheming"	The duke is a jealous, egotistical character.

Try It

Read the passage. As you read, underline key plot details or dialogue that might help you support an analysis of the story. Use the questions to help you.

excerpted and adapted from

Little Women

by Louisa May Alcott

As the girls gathered about the table, Mrs. March said, with a particularly happy face, "I've got a treat for you after supper."

A quick, bright smile went round like a streak of sunshine. Beth clapped her hands, regardless of the biscuit she held, and Jo tossed up her napkin, crying, "A letter! A letter! Three cheers for Father!"

> What evidence from the passage shows that the girls are anxious to hear from their father?

"Yes, a nice long letter. He is well, and thinks he shall get through the cold season better than we feared. He sends all sorts of loving wishes for Christmas, and a special message to you girls," said Mrs. March, patting her pocket as if she had got a treasure there.

"Hurry and get done! Don't stop to quirk your little finger and simper over your plate, Amy," cried Jo, choking on her tea and dropping her bread, butter side down, on the carpet in her haste to get at the treat.

Beth ate no more, but crept away to sit in her shadowy corner and brood over the delight to come, till the others were ready.

They all drew to the fire, Mother in the big chair with Beth at her feet, Meg and Amy perched on either arm of the chair, and Jo leaning on the back, where no one would see any sign of emotion if the letter should happen to be touching. Very few letters were written in those hard times that were not touching, especially those which fathers sent home. In this one little was said of the hardships endured, the dangers faced, or the homesickness conquered. It was a cheerful, hopeful letter, full of lively descriptions of camp life, marches, and military news, and only at the end did the writer's heart overflow with fatherly love and longing for the little girls at home.

Continued on the next page ▶

Continued from the previous page

"Give them all of my dear love and a kiss. Tell them I think of them by day, pray for them by night, and find my best comfort in their affection at all times. I know they will remember all I said to them, that they will be loving children to you, will do their duty faithfully, fight their bosom enemies bravely, and conquer themselves so beautifully that when I come back to them I may be fonder and prouder than ever of my little women." Everybody sniffed when they came to that part. Jo wasn't ashamed of the great tear that dropped off the end of her nose, and Amy never minded the rumpling of her curls as she hid her face on her mother's shoulder.

"I'll try and be what he loves to call me, 'a little woman' and not be rough and wild, but do my duty here instead of wanting to be somewhere else," said Jo, thinking that keeping her temper at home was a much harder task than facing a rebel or two down South.

What kind of person is Jo?

What evidence from the passage tells you that Mr. March is fighting in the Civil War?

HOTS Analyze

Are the Marches a very close family? How do you know?

Apply It

Read the passage. As you read, pay attention to key plot details or dialogue that might help you support an analysis of the story. Answer the questions that follow.

excerpted and adapted from

The Red Badge of Courage
by Stephen Crane

When he had stood in the doorway with his soldier's clothes on his back, and with the light of excitement and expectancy in his eyes almost defeating the glow of regret for the home bonds, he had seen two tears leaving their trails on his mother's scarred cheeks.

Still, she had disappointed him by saying nothing whatever about returning with his shield or on it. He had privately primed himself for a beautiful scene. He had prepared certain sentences that he thought could be used with touching effect. But her words destroyed his plans. She had doggedly peeled potatoes and addressed him as follows: "You watch out, Henry, and take good care of yourself in this here fighting business— you watch out, and take good care of yourself. Don't go a-thinking you can lick the whole rebel army at the start, because you can't. You're just one little fellow amongst a hell lot of others, and you've got to keep quiet and do what they tell you. I know how you are, Henry.

"I've knitted you eight pair of socks, Henry, and I've put in all your best shirts, because I want my boy to be just as warm and comfortable as anybody in the army. Whenever they get holes in them, I want you to send them right-away back to me, so I can darn them.

"And always be careful and choose your company. There are lots of bad men in the army, Henry. The army makes them wild, and they like nothing better than the job of leading off a young fellow like you, as you've never been away from home much and has always had a mother, and a-learning them to drink and swear. Keep clear of them folks, Henry. I don't want you to ever do anything, Henry, that you would be ashamed to let me know about. Just think as if I was a-watching you. If you keep that in your mind always, I guess you'll come out about right.

Continued on the next page ➡

Continued from the previous page

"You must always remember your father, too, child, and remember he never drunk a drop of liquor in his life, and seldom swore a cross oath.

"I don't know what else to tell you, Henry, except that you must never do no shirking, child, on my account. If so be a time comes when you have to be killed or do a mean thing, why, Henry, don't think of anything except what's right, because there's many a woman has to bear up against such things these times, and the Lord will take care of us all.

"Don't forget about the socks and the shirts, child; and I've put a cup of blackberry jam with your bundle, because I know you like it above all things. Good-bye, Henry. Watch out, and be a good boy."

Answer these questions about "The Red Badge of Courage." Write your answers in complete sentences.

1. What evidence in the passage reveals that this will be the first time that Henry is leaving home?

_____

_____

2. What evidence in the passage shows that Henry and his mother have different views about his decision to go to war?

_____

_____

3. How does the dialogue in this passage support the conclusion that Henry and his mother are poor?

_____

_____

4. One of the major themes of "The Red Badge of Courage" is that the reality of war does not live up to the way it is idealized. How could this passage support that analysis?

_____

_____

_____

_____

Theme

Learn About It

Theme refers to the overall message of a story. Though it is one of the most important parts of a story, the theme is rarely stated directly in its text. Instead, it is something the reader determines by figuring out how all of the different elements of a work of fiction—plot, language, and characters—relate to events in the real world. Themes can come in the form of a moral, a lesson, or a general statement about life. While short stories generally have one main theme, longer works such as novels and dramas can have many themes.

Read the passage. As you read, try to connect the events in the story to events in the real world, or to your own personal experience.

adapted from
The Dog and the Reflection
by Aesop

A dog, crossing a bridge over a stream with a piece of meat in his mouth, saw his own reflection in the water and took it for that of another dog, with a piece of meat double his own in size. He immediately let go of his own, and fiercely attacked the other dog to get the larger piece from him. In doing so, the dog lost both: that which he grasped at in the water, because it was a shadow; and his own, because the stream swept it away.

Events in the Story	Connection to the Real World	Theme
Dog already has enough food, tries to steal from another dog to get more food, ends up losing everything.	People who are greedy often end up losing the things that are the most important in life.	Sometimes it is best to be satisfied with what you have.

Try It

Read the passage. As you read, circle details that relate to real life or your own personal experience. Use the questions to help you.

excerpted and adapted from

The Fir Tree

by Hans Christian Andersen

Far down in the forest, where the sun is warm and the air is fresh, grew a pretty little fir tree; and yet it was not happy, for it wished so much to be tall like its companions. As it grew, it would complain, "How I wish I were as tall as the other trees, then my top would overlook the wide world." The tree was so discontented that it took no pleasure in the warm sunshine, the birds, or the clouds that floated over it every day.

In autumn, the woodcutters came and cut down several of the tallest trees, and the young fir tree, which was now grown to its full height, looked on with great interest. The trees were placed upon wagons, and taken out of the forest. "Where were they going?"

> What is the fir tree's main character trait in this story?

A bird answered, "They are being made into great ships, to sail on the sea."

"Oh, how I wish I were tall enough to go on the sea," said the fir tree.

"Never mind the sea," said the sun. "Rejoice in your youth, and the life you have in this beautiful forest." But still the tree longed for more.

> How does the fir tree's character affect the theme of the story?

Christmastime drew near, and many young trees were cut down, and were likewise dragged out of the forest.

"Where are they going?" asked the fir tree. "They are not taller than I am. What were they chosen for?"

The bird answered, "I have seen such trees in the windows of the houses in the town. They are dressed up in the most splendid manner, and children sing and dance around them."

"That sounds wonderful!" thought the fir tree. "It would be much better than crossing the sea. Oh! I wish I were standing in that warm room, with all that happiness around me!"

"Be happy with us," said the air and the sunlight. "Enjoy your own bright life in the fresh air." But the tree was not happy, though it stood fair and tall in the light of the sun.

Continued on the next page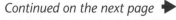

17

Continued from the previous page

The following Christmas, the discontented fir tree was the first to fall. It felt pain at being cut down, and sorrow at leaving its forest home. It knew that it should never again see its friends the trees, the birds, or the sun.

What lesson does the fir tree learn at the end of the story?

After a long journey, it was placed in a large room in a great house, where it was dressed in garlands and lights, with a great star upon its head. Children came and sang and danced around it. It was the proudest the fir tree had ever been. But the night passed, and soon after the tree was dragged out into the yard, where its once beautiful leaves withered and yellowed.

As the fir lay on the cold ground, it thought, "Oh, how I long for the wood where the sun shines and the birds sing. Those were happy days! I wish I had enjoyed them more, but now it is too late."

HOTS Analyze

What other characters have you read about that remind you of the fir tree? Did they learn similar lessons?

Apply It

Read the passage. As you read, ask yourself questions about how the plot and characters contribute to the theme. Answer the questions that follow.

excerpted and adapted from

The King of the Polar Bears

by L. Frank Baum

The King of the Polar Bears lived among the icebergs in the far north country. His huge body was covered with long, white hair that glistened like silver, and his claws were razor sharp. His subjects feared his size and strength, but loved him for his wisdom and kindness.

One day, he emerged from his cave and saw a boat approaching. In the boat were men. When the great bear came to the water's edge to greet them, a man stood up in the boat and with a strange instrument made a loud "bang!" The polar bear felt a shock, fell upon the hard ice, and fainted.

When he awoke he was shivering and in pain, for the men had cut away his glorious coat and carried it with them. A group of gulls flying overhead saw the king upon the ground, and their leader said, "The king suffers for lack of covering. Let us give him as many of our feathers as we can spare." One by one they plucked the softest feathers from under their wings, and dropped them upon his body, saying, "Courage, friend! Our feathers will guard you from the cold winds."

But when the king returned to his cavern and the other bears saw his body covered with feathers, they were horrified. One of them, a warrior named Woof, said, "A bear with feathers is no bear at all, and our king must resemble the rest of us. I will fight him, and then I will reign as king." The other bears growled their agreement. Mustering all of his pride, the king accepted this challenge.

Then he visited his friends, the gulls, and told them of the coming battle. "I shall conquer," he said, proudly. "Yet my people are right— only a hairy one like themselves can command their obedience."

Continued on the next page ➤

19

Continued from the previous page

The leader of the gulls said, "One of our number flew to the city of men and came upon a coat so great in size that it must be yours. I will send a hundred of my gulls to the city to bring it back to you."

The day of the great battle came, but the gulls had not yet returned from their errand. The king was disappointed, but he resolved to fight bravely without his coat. He advanced to the opening of his cavern, where he was met by an assembly of bears, with Woof at their head. "Come nearer, bird-bear!" Woof cried. "Come nearer, that I may pluck your feathers!"

This defiance filled the king with rage. He ruffled his feathers as a bird does, charged forward, and felled Woof with one mighty blow.

While the other bears stood looking on with fear and wonder, the sky grew dark. A hundred gulls flew down and draped the king's recovered coat over his shoulders. And behold! The bears saw before them the well-known form of their master, and bowed their heads in homage to the mighty King of the Polar Bears.

Answer these questions about "The King of the Polar Bears." Write your answers in complete sentences.

1. What is the source of the conflict between the king and the other bears?

   _____

   _____

2. How is this conflict resolved?

   _____

   _____

3. What message can a reader take away from this resolution?

   _____

   _____

4. Even though characters in this story are animals, they speak and act like people. Think about the bears' reaction to the king after he loses his coat. How might this be a comment on the way people treat one another?

   _____

   _____

5. Throughout the story, Woof is arrogant and disrespectful toward the king. Considering what happens to him at the end, what do you think the author might be trying to say about this kind of attitude?

   _____

   _____

6. Consider the way humans treat animals in this story. What do you think the author might be trying to say about how humans interact with nature?

   _____

   _____

Summarize Text

Learn About It

When you **summarize** a passage, you express its overall meaning as concisely as possible. There are several strategies you can use to summarize a work of fiction. In some cases, you can break a passage into smaller sections, determine the main idea of each, and then identify a connection between these sections. For longer works of fiction, it might be easier to identify the main characters, action, conflict, and resolution, and then write one or two sentences explaining how these different elements are connected in a story.

Read the following summary of "The Bat, the Birds, and the Beasts" by Aesop. As you read, pay attention to how it focuses on the main aspects of the story.

A great battle was about to happen between the Birds and the Beasts. The Bat did not know which side to join. When the Birds invited the Bat to join them, he declined claiming he was a Beast. When the Beasts asked the Bat to join them, he declined claiming that he was a Bird. Peace was made between the Birds and the Beasts before a battle could happen. Each group had a party to celebrate. When the Bat tried to enter a party, he was turned away because he was not part of that group.

Summary: The Bat does not choose sides before a battle. After peace is declared, neither group lets the Bat join in the celebration.

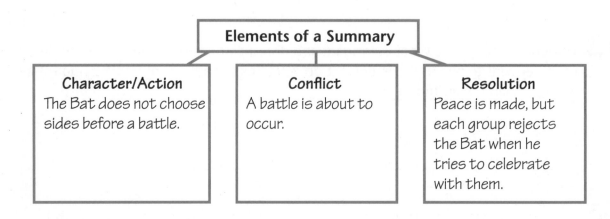

Elements of a Summary

Character/Action	Conflict	Resolution
The Bat does not choose sides before a battle.	A battle is about to occur.	Peace is made, but each group rejects the Bat when he tries to celebrate with them.

Try It

Read the passage. As you read, underline the main idea of each paragraph.
Circle important details to include in a summary. Use the questions to help you.

excerpted and adapted from

The Adventures of Tom Sawyer
by Mark Twain

Huckleberry Finn, the juvenile outlaw of the town, was dreaded by all the mothers of the town, because he was idle and lawless and vulgar and bad—and because all their children admired him so, and wished to be like him. Tom Sawyer was like the rest of the respectable boys, in that he envied Huckleberry as a flamboyant outcast, and was under strict orders not to play with him. So, of course, he played with him every time he got a chance. Huckleberry was always dressed in the cast-off clothes of full-grown men, and they were fluttering with rags. His hat was a vast ruin with a wide crescent cut out of its brim, and his coat, when he wore one, hung nearly to his heels. Only one suspender supported his pants; the seat of the pants hung low, and the fringed legs dragged in the dirt when not rolled up.

Huckleberry came and went, at his own free will. He slept on doorsteps in fine weather and in empty sheds in wet; he did not have to go to school, or call any being master or obey anybody; he could go fishing or swimming when and where he chose, and stay as long as it suited him; nobody forbade him to fight; he could sit up as late as he pleased; he was always the first boy that went barefoot in the spring and the last to wear shoes in the fall; he never had to wash, nor put on clean clothes. In a word, everything that goes to make life precious that boy had. So thought every harassed, hampered, respectable boy in St. Petersburg.

> What do the first two paragraphs tell you about Huckleberry Finn?

Continued on the next page ➤

Continued from the previous page

When Huck came under the protection of the Widow Douglas, she introduced him into society, and his sufferings were almost more than he could bear. The widow's servants kept him clean and neat, and they bedded him nightly in sheets that had not one little spot or stain. He had to eat with a knife and fork; he had to use napkin, cup, and plate; he had to read books; he had to talk properly. Wherever he turned, the bars and shackles of civilization shut him in and bound him hand and foot.

> **What information are you given in the last two paragraphs?**

He bravely bore his miseries three weeks, and then one day turned up missing. For forty-eight hours the widow hunted for him everywhere. Early the third morning Tom Sawyer wisely went poking behind the abandoned slaughterhouse, where he found the refugee. Huck had slept there; he had just breakfasted upon some stolen food, and was lying now in comfort. He was unkempt, uncombed, and clad in the same old ruin of rags from the days when he was free and happy. Tom told him the trouble he had been causing, and in the end convinced him to go home.

> **What information would you not include in a summary?**

How would you summarize this passage?

Apply It

Read the passage. As you read, pay attention to the characters and plot details. Answer the questions that follow.

adapted from

Three Questions
by Leo Tolstoy

It once occurred to a king, that if he always knew the right time to begin everything; if he always knew the right people to listen to; and if he always knew the most important thing to do, he would never fail in anything. The king proclaimed that he would give a great reward to anyone who could answer his questions about how to achieve these three things. Many learned men came before the king and offered their ideas, but none satisfied him.

Undeterred, the king decided to disguise himself and seek out a wise and famous hermit. When the king found him, the hermit was digging the ground in front of his hut. Seeing the king, the hermit greeted him and went on digging. The hermit was frail and weak, and breathed heavily as he dug.

The king went up to him and said: "I have come to you to ask you three questions: How can I learn to do the right thing at the right time? Who are the people I most need? And, what affairs are the most important?"

The hermit gave no answer, but just continued digging.

"You are tired," said the king. "Let me take the spade and work a while for you."

The king labored until sunset, when a wounded man came running out of the woods and collapsed. The king and the hermit dressed the man's wounds and laid him down in the hermit's hut. The king, exhausted from his own labor, soon fell asleep as well. When he awoke, he saw the wounded man standing over him.

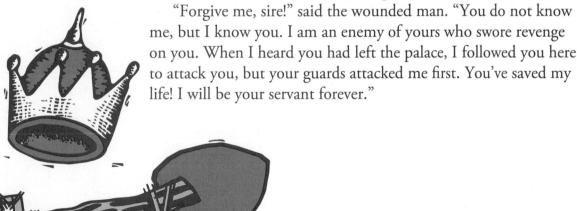

"Forgive me, sire!" said the wounded man. "You do not know me, but I know you. I am an enemy of yours who swore revenge on you. When I heard you had left the palace, I followed you here to attack you, but your guards attacked me first. You've saved my life! I will be your servant forever."

Continued on the next page ➡

Continued from the previous page

The king was glad to have made peace with his enemy, and promised to reward him for his faithfulness.

Finding the hermit outside his hut, the king once again pressed him:

"For the last time, I pray you to answer my questions, wise man."

"You have already been answered!" said the hermit. "If you had not dug for me, but had gone your way, that man would have attacked you. So the most important time was when you were digging the beds for me; I was the most important man and helping me was your most important business. When that man ran to us, the most important time was when you were attending to him, and he was the most important man, and what you did for him was your most important business. Remember then: the only time that is important is now, because it is the only time when we have any power. The most necessary person is whom you are with, and the most important affair is to bring about good, because for that is the main purpose of this life!"

Answer these questions about "Three Questions." Write your answers in complete sentences.

1. Who is the main character of this story?

_____

_____

2. What is the main character of this story looking for?

_____

_____

3. What conflict does the main character encounter?

_____

_____

4. How is this conflict resolved?

_____

_____

5. Review your answers for the previous four questions, and summarize the entire passage in one or two sentences.

_____

_____

_____

_____

Drawing and Supporting Inferences

Learn About It

Sometimes a writer will leave certain details out of a story to make it more dramatic or humorous. In these cases, it is up to readers to draw their own conclusions based on the information given in the story. These conclusions are known as inferences. To make an **inference**, use what you read about the characters and plot details, combined with common sense and your own experience, to fill in the missing details.

Read the passage. As you read, pay attention to the details in the passage. Draw an inference based on details in the passage.

Ben's community library was sponsoring an art contest, and Ben wanted to bring his imaginary character, Crater Carl, to life. Ben decided to make a comic book of Carl's adventures.

Ben preferred to work late at night, when he could gaze at the moon and imagine Carl's swashbuckling adventures. After three days of imagining and drawing, Ben gingerly placed the comic in an envelope and nervously mailed it to his local library.

Details from the Story	Common Sense/ Your Experience	Inference
Ben creates an imaginary character. Ben makes a comic book. Ben gingerly places the comic book in an envelope and nervously mails it.	It takes a lot of creativity to make a comic book. People get nervous during a contest or competition.	Ben has a great imagination. Ben is excited about the contest.

Try It

Read the passage. As you read, underline the details that support any inferences you draw. Use the questions to help you.

adapted from

The Open Window

by H. H. Munro

In an attempt to calm Framton Nuttel's fragile nerves, his psychiatrist recommended that he spend some time in the country. One October afternoon, he called upon his new neighbor, Mrs. Sappleton, to introduce himself. Upon arriving, he was greeted by her niece Vera, a young lady of fifteen.

"My aunt will be down shortly, Mr. Nuttel," said Vera. "Do you know anyone around here?"

"Hardly a soul," said Framton.

"Then you know nothing about my aunt's tragedy?"

"Her tragedy?" asked Framton.

"You may wonder why we keep that window open," said the niece, indicating a large window that opened on to a lawn. "Three years ago, her husband and her two young brothers went hunting with their white spaniel. They never came back, and are presumed to have drowned in a nearby swamp. Poor aunt never recovered. She still thinks that they will return someday, which is why the window is kept open every evening until dusk. Sometimes on evenings like this, I get a creepy feeling that they will all walk in through that window—"

It was a relief to Framton when the aunt bustled into the room and apologized for being late.

"I hope you don't mind the open window," said Mrs. Sappleton. "My husband and brothers will soon be home from hunting, and they always come in this way."

As she chatted cheerfully about her husband's prospects for hunting season, Framton tried to turn the conversation to a less uncomfortable topic. As they spoke, he noticed that her eyes were constantly straying past him to the open window and the lawn beyond.

> What can you infer about Framton's personality? Use evidence from the passage to support your inference.

> What does Framton think about Mrs. Sappleton when she says her husband and brothers would be returning home?

> What do the developments in the last few paragraphs allow you to infer about Vera's personality?

Continued on the next page ➤

Continued from the previous page

"Here they are at last!" she cried. "Just in time for tea!"

Framton shivered slightly and turned towards the niece with a look intended to convey sympathetic comprehension. The child was staring out through the open window with a dazed horror in her eyes. Framton swung round in his seat and looked in the same direction. In the deepening twilight, three ghostly, muddy figures, one wearing a white coat, were walking across the lawn toward the window, as a small white spaniel trotted at their heels.

Pale with terror, Framton grabbed at his coat and hat and bounded headlong for the door.

"Hello, my dear," said the man in the white coat, coming in through the window, "Who was that who bolted out as we came up?"

"A most peculiar man, a Mr. Nuttel," said Mrs. Sappleton. "He dashed off without a word of goodbye when you arrived. One would think he had seen a ghost."

"I expect it was the spaniel," said the niece calmly. "He told me he had a horror of dogs. He was once hunted by a pack of wild dogs, and had to spend the night in a newly dug grave with the creatures snarling just above him. Enough to make anyone lose their nerve."

Drama at short notice was Vera's specialty.

HOTS Analyze

What information from the text allows you to infer that Vera is playing a trick on Framton?

Apply It

Read the passage. As you read, pay attention to the title, plot, dialogue, and characters, and use these details to make inferences about any missing information. Answer the questions that follow.

adapted from
The Story of the Vanishing Patient
by Elia W. Peattie

There had always been strange stories circulating about the Netherton's house. Everyone in the neighborhood thought it strange that they lived there so little. They were nearly always traveling, and when they did come home, it was only to entertain a number of guests from the city.

Dr. Block and his wife lived next door to the Nethertons, though "next door" was still quite a walk. One night, after Dr. Block's last patient left, and he and his wife were ready to settle down for the evening, the doorbell rang. The young physician went downstairs. At the door stood a man whom he had never seen before.

"My wife is lying very ill next door," said the stranger. "Will you please come to her at once?"

"Next door?" cried the physician. "I didn't know the Nethertons were home!"

"Please! Hurry!" begged the man.

The doctor's wife protested when she heard the story. "There is no one at the Nethertons'. I sit where I can see the front door, and haven't seen anyone come or go all day. I have a bad feeling about this—don't go."

"But I'm the only doctor around for miles. I have to."

At the head of the stairs the man met him. He motioned the physician to follow him, and the two went down the hall to a spacious and comfortable front room. On a silken couch, in the midst of pillows, lay a sick woman. Dr. Block asked a few questions. The man answered them and the woman remained silent. The physician wrote a prescription, which he left on the mantle on his way out of the room.

The next morning, before breakfast, the doctor strode over to the Nethertons' house to check on his patient. He found the front door locked, and received no replies to his repeated knocking. The old gardener who lived in a cottage on the grounds was cutting the grass near at hand, and he came running up.

Continued on the next page ➡

Continued from the previous page

"What you knocking for, doctor?" said he. "The folks ain't come home yet. There ain't nobody there."

"But I was called here last night. A man came for me to attend to his sick wife. Could you let me in?"

Hearing this, the old gardener shivered.

"You mean you saw them?" whispered he, with chattering teeth. "Don't you never go in there, doctor! And if anyone ever summons you there, don't follow!"

Dr. Block took the bunch of keys from the old man's pocket and himself unlocked the front door and entered. The place was silent and vacant; dust lay all over the furniture, even the silk couch. The air was musty, as though the room had not been used for a long time. But on the mantle was the prescription that the doctor had written the night before.

When he told his wife, she kissed him and said:

"Next time when I tell you to stay at home, you must stay!"

Answer these questions about "The Story of the Vanishing Patient." Write your answers in complete sentences.

1. What can you infer about the setting of this story?

_____

_____

2. What details from the passage allow you to make this inference?

_____

_____

3. What can you infer about the couple the doctor visits at the Nethertons' house?

_____

_____

4. What details from the text allowed you to make this inference?

_____

_____

5. How could the title help support this inference?

_____

_____

6. What details from the text would allow you to infer that the old gardener had encountered the couple before?

_____

_____

Figurative Language and Connotative Meanings

Learn About It

Figurative language refers to a set of literary techniques that allows writers to go beyond the literal definitions of words to give their writing a deeper meaning. A **metaphor** is a comparison that shows how two dissimilar things resemble each other. A **simile** is a comparison that uses the words *like* or *as*. **Personification** is a literary device in which an object or idea is described as having human qualities. A word can carry a **connotative** meaning which is an implied meaning different from the word's literal meaning.

Read the poem. As you read, pay attention to the author's use of figurative language.

adapted from

A Book

by Emily Dickinson

There is no vessel like a book
To take us lands away,
Nor any racehorse like a page
Of prancing poetry.
This travel may the poorest take
Without paying a toll;
How cheaply comes the chariot
That bears a human soul!

Similes
There is no vessel like a book
Nor any racehorse like a page

Metaphors
This travel may the poorest take
How cheaply comes the chariot

Meaning
A book is the best way
to be transported to
another place or time.

Try It

Read the passage. As you read, underline examples of figurative language.
Use the questions to help you.

excerpted and adapted from

The Outcast
by Boleslaw Prus

The river Bialka springs from under a hill no bigger than a cottage; the water murmurs in its little hollow like a swarm of bees getting ready for their flight.

For the distance of fifteen miles, the Bialka flows on level ground. Woods, villages, and trees in the fields show up clearly and become smaller and smaller as they recede into the distance. It is a bit of country like a round table on which human beings live like a butterfly covered by a blue flower. What man finds and what another leaves him he may eat, but he must not go too far or fly too high.

Fifteen to twenty miles farther to the south, the country begins to change. The shallow banks of the Bialka rise and retreat from each other; the flat fields rise, and the path leads ever more frequently and steeply up and down hill.

The plain has disappeared and given place to a ravine; you are surrounded by hills of the height of a many-storied house; all are covered with bushes; sometimes the ascent is steep, sometimes gradual. The first ravine leads into a second, wilder and narrower, and then into a succession of nine or ten. Cold and dampness cling to you when you walk through them; you climb one of the hills and find yourself surrounded by a network of forking and winding ravines.

A short distance from the riverbanks the landscape is again quite different. The hills grow smaller and stand separate like great anthills. You have emerged from the country of ravines into the broad valley of the Bialka, and the bright sun shines full into your eyes.

> Pay attention to the first two paragraphs of this passage. How does the author use simile to describe the region surrounding the Bialka?

> A simile is a comparison that uses *like* or *as*. A metaphor makes a comparison without using these words.

> What does the phrase "cold and dampness cling to you" connote?

Continued on the next page ➤

35

Continued from the previous page

If the earth is a table on which Providence has spread a banquet for creation, then the valley of the Bialka is a gigantic, long-shaped dish with upturned rim. In the winter this dish is white, but at other seasons it is like a patchwork of colors, with forms severe and irregular, but beautiful. The Divine Potter has placed a field at the bottom of the dish and cut it through from north to south with the ribbon of the Bialka sparkling with waves of sapphire blue in the morning, crimson in the evening, golden at midday, and silver in moonlit nights.

When He had formed the bottom, the Great Potter shaped the rim, taking care that each side should possess an individual character.

The west bank is wild; the field touches the steep gravel hills, where a few scattered hawthorn bushes and dwarf birches grow. Patches of earth show here and there, as though the turf had been peeled. Even the hardiest plants eschew these patches, where instead of vegetation the surface presents clay and strata of sand, or else rock showing its teeth to the green field.

HOTS Analyze

Throughout the passage, the author uses metaphors to compare the region surrounding the Bialka to a table, a banquet, and a dish. What message about the area do you think the author is trying to convey?

Apply It

Read the poem. As you read, pay attention to the figurative and connotative meanings of the language. Answer the questions that follow.

adapted from

The Last Leaf

by Oliver Wendell Holmes

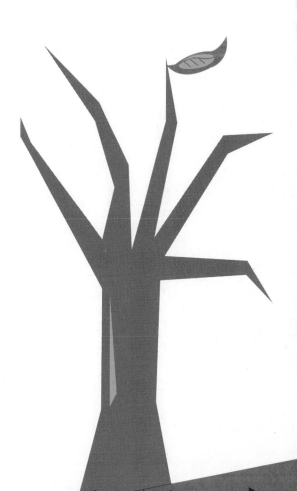

I saw him once before,
As he passed by the door;
    And again
The pavement stones resound,
5   As he limps all over the ground
    With his cane.

They say that in his prime,
Before the sharp knife of Time
    Cut him down,
10   Not a better man was found
By the postman on his rounds
    Through the town.

But now he walks the streets,
And he looks at all he meets
15   Sad and wan;
And shakes his feeble head,
That it seems as if he said,
    "They are gone."

My grandmamma has said—
20   Poor old lady, she is dead
    Long ago—
That he had a Roman nose,
And his cheek was like a rose
    In the snow.

Continued on the next page ➤

Continued from the previous page

25 But now his nose is thin,
   And it rests upon his chin
     Like a staff;
   And a crook is in his back,
   And a melancholy crack
30   In his laugh.

   I know it is a sin
   For me to sit and grin
     At him here;
   But the old three-cornered hat,
35 And the breeches and all that,
     Are so weird!

   And if I should live to be
   The last leaf upon the tree
     In the spring,
40 Let them smile, as I do now,
   At the old forsaken bough
     Where I cling.

Answer these questions about "The Last Leaf." Write your answers in complete sentences.

1. What is an example of personification in the second stanza?

   _____

   _____

2. Consider the author's description of how the old man walked in the first stanza. How does a simile in the fifth stanza relate to this description?

   _____

   _____

3. When the author writes that the old man's cheeks were once "like a rose / in the snow," what is he saying about the old man's appearance in his youth?

   _____

   _____

4. In the last stanza of the poem, what metaphor does the author use to describe people's lives?

   _____

   _____

5. What does this metaphor convey about the nature of life?

   _____

   _____

6. Why did the author use the word *melancholy* to describe the old man's laugh?

   _____

   _____

Point of View and Dramatic Irony

Learn About It

> **Point of view** is the perspective of a story's or poem's narrator. **First-person** point of view tells a story from the narrator's perspective, using the pronoun *I*. **Third-person** point of view tells a story from an outside perspective. **Objective** third-person narrators can only describe events as they perceive them, but **omniscient** third-person narrators can relate the thoughts and feelings of all of the characters in a story. The narrator's point of view can often be used to affect the reader's expectations about how a particular situation might be resolved. When the outcome is different from what one would normally expect, this is known as **irony**. **Dramatic irony** is when the audience or reader is aware of plot details that are kept hidden from certain characters.

Read the passage. As you read, pay attention to the narrator's point of view, and look for elements of irony.

Jesse could not wait for summer to begin. When the final bell rang on the last day of that long school year, he sprinted for the door, past his classmates, past his teacher, and past the "CAUTION: WET FLOOR" sign that the janitor had just posted.

"You took a nasty spill there," said the doctor as he set the cast on Jesse's forearm. "Now, you'll have to keep this cast on for about six weeks, and make sure you don't get it wet. The good news is that we'll have it off right before school starts in September."

CAUTION

WET FLOOR

What Jesse Expected	What Actually Happened
To enjoy summer after a long school year	Jesse broke his wrist rushing out of school, meaning he'll have to spend summer with his wrist in a cast.

Try It

Read the passage. Pay attention to how the point of view affects your reading of the passage, and circle examples of irony. Use the questions to help you.

adapted from

The Gift of the Magi
by O. Henry

Three times Della counted her savings, and each time received the same result: $1.87. She cried softly as she looked out at the gray December afternoon. Tomorrow would be Christmas Day, yet she could not buy her husband Jim a present. She had been saving every penny she could for months, longing for the day when she could give him something worthy of his love for her, and of hers for him. Turning her gaze from the window, Della set her eyes upon a nearby mirror, when she was seized by a sudden inspiration that at once gladdened and terrified her.

Though poor, Jim and Della possessed two things that made them the envy of their neighbors. One was Jim's priceless gold watch. The other was Della's hair, which was so long, silky, and beautiful, it almost made itself a garment on her. Seeing how it fell upon her shoulders, she realized what she could do to get the money for Jim's present. Wiping away a reluctant tear, she threw on her coat and hat and hurried out to Mrs. Sofronie's Wig Shop.

"Will you buy my hair?" asked Della.

"Twenty dollars," said Mrs. Sofronie, lifting her scissors with a practiced hand.

"Give it to me quick," said Della.

With hardly a thought for the mound of beautiful hair left on Mrs. Sofronie's floor, Della leapt from her chair and hurried out to find Jim's present. And find it she did: a gold watch chain, perfect for Jim's beloved watch. When Della reached home and saw herself at the mirror, she was shocked by the sight of her short hair. She busied herself curling what was left of it, when the door opened and Jim stepped in. As he set his eyes on Della, a peculiar expression fell across his face.

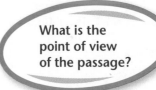

What is the point of view of the passage?

Continued on the next page ➡

Continued from the previous page

"Jim, darling," she cried, "don't look at me that way. I had my hair cut off and sold because I needed the money for your Christmas present."

Jim snapped out of his momentary trance and embraced Della. "Don't make any mistake, Dell," he said, "I don't think there's anything in the way of a haircut that could make me love you any less. But if you'll unwrap that package you may see why you had me confused at first."

Della opened her gift, and let out a scream of joy that soon turned to tears. For there lay a set of expensive combs that Della had long yearned for, but never hoped she could have. And now, they were hers, but her hair was gone. Still, she was able to look up with a smile and say: "My hair grows so fast, Jim!" Then she leaped up to hand Jim his present.

"Isn't it great, Jim? I hunted all over town to find it. Give me your watch. I want to see how it looks."

Jim tumbled down on the couch and put his hands under the back of his head and smiled. "Della," said he, "let's put our Christmas presents away and keep them a while. We won't really be able to use them just at present. I sold the watch to get the money to buy your combs."

> **What is ironic about the end of the passage?**

How does point of view affect dramatic irony?

Apply It

Read the drama. Ask yourself questions about point of view and irony and how they function in this story. Answer the questions that follow.

excerpted and adapted from

Cyrano de Bergerac
by Edmond Rostand

Setting: Outside Roxane's house at nighttime. Enter CHRISTIAN and CYRANO, beneath Roxane's balcony.

CHRISTIAN: You have to help me, Cyrano!

CYRANO: What can I do?

CHRISTIAN: I cannot live unless I can get Roxane to fall in love with me again! Teach me how to be eloquent like you are!

CYRANO: Here? Right now?

The light goes on in Roxane's window.

CHRISTIAN: (*loudly*) There she is! What am I going to do? What am I supposed to say?

CYRANO: Ssshh! Be quiet! I think I have an idea. I'll hide beneath the balcony and whisper to you what you should say to Roxane.

ROXANE: (*opening her window*) Who's down there?

CHRISTIAN: (*clears his throat*) It is I, Christian.

ROXANE: (*disdainfully*) Oh. You again? Go away! I don't want to speak to you.

CHRISTIAN: Please! Listen to me!

ROXANE: I don't want to speak to you. You don't love me any more!

CHRISTIAN: (*saying the words that CYRANO whispers to him*) You're right. I don't just love you *any*more, I love you *ever*more!

ROXANE: (*about to close her window, but pauses*) Hmm, I've never heard you talk like that before....

CHRISTIAN: (*as before, saying the words that CYRANO whispers to him*) Love grows and struggles in me like . . . an angry child . . . that rocks my heart . . . like a cradle....

ROXANE: (*coming out on the balcony*) I never knew you were such a poet! But why are you speaking so slowly?

Continued on the next page ▶

Continued from the previous page

CYRANO (*pushes CHRISTIAN under the balcony, and stands in his place*) Here—you're taking too long—she'll find us out! Let me do it!

ROXANE: Is someone down there with you? Why haven't you answered me?

CYRANO: (*in a low voice, imitating CHRISTIAN*) If I speak slowly, it is because I, in darkness, am awed by the light that shines from you.

ROXANE: Oh, Christian, I never knew you could be so romantic! Let me come down to you!

CYRANO: (*quickly, again imitating Christian*) No!

ROXANE: (*points out the bench under the balcony*) Well, stand over on that bench so I can see you!

CYRANO: No!

ROXANE: What? Why not?

CYRANO: Let me enjoy my one chance to speak to you . . . unseen! Only let me ask one thing more….

CHRISTIAN: (*under the balcony*) Yes! A kiss!

ROXANE: (*startled*) A kiss?

CYRANO: (*to CHRISTIAN*) Be quiet! You'll ruin everything!

ROXANE: (*leaning over*) Are you talking to someone down there?

CYRANO: Myself! I was, uh, angry with myself for being too forward!

ROXANE: (*hearing a noise from within*) Someone's coming! I have to go—come back to me soon, my dear Christian!

She closes her window and turns off the light.

CHRISTIAN: (*emerging from under the balcony*) Cyrano—that was amazing! You'll win me that kiss yet!

CYRANO: (*hiding his resentment*) Well, you're on your own from here.

CHRISTIAN: Sooner or later, Roxane will be mine again!

CYRANO: That is true. Sooner or later, it will be so, because you are young, and she is beautiful. (*to himself*) It will be Christian, but how I wish it were me instead!

Answer these questions about "Cyrano de Bergerac." Write your answers in complete sentences.

1. What are two examples of dramatic irony in this scene?

_____

_____

2. How do Cyrano's words and actions heighten the irony of the scene?

_____

_____

3. How does the setting and staging contribute to the level of dramatic irony of this scene?

_____

_____

4. If the events of this story were told from Roxane's point of view, would the tension and irony of this scene be increased or decreased? Why?

_____

_____

5. If this story were told as an omniscient third-person narrative instead of as a drama, how would that change the way the events are presented?

_____

_____

Word Choice and Tone

Learn About It

> **Tone** refers to the author's attitude toward the subject of a work of fiction. An author's tone is reflected by his or her **word choice**. An author will use positive words and phrases to set a happy or inspiring tone for a work of fiction, and negative words to set a sad or harsh tone. Words with no emotional content create a neutral tone.

Read the passage. Notice the tone.

Emma awoke with a startle. Tree branches crashed against the window, creating a terrible racket. She switched on the light—nothing. Her heart beat rapidly as she realized there was no electricity! What a time for her parents to have to go to Grandma's.

Trying to remain calm, Emma looked out the window. Wind and rain were whipping wires and branches around. Her parents had told her what to do in a big storm, but now her mind was totally blank.

Tone	serious
Word choice	branches crashed, terrible racket, heart beat rapidly, no electricity, whipping wires, mind was totally blank

Try It

Read the passage. As you read, underline words that reflect the author's attitude to the subject of this passage. Use the questions to help you.

excerpted and adapted from

The Strange Case of Dr. Jekyll and Mr. Hyde
by Robert Louis Stevenson

Mr. Utterson waited outside the residence of his client Dr. Jekyll, keeping an appointment they had made to discuss the latter's will. Dr. Jekyll had as yet not appeared, but as Utterson waited, he could hear the steps of another figure approaching. The steps drew swiftly nearer, and swelled out suddenly louder as they turned the end of the street. Mr. Utterson, looking forth from the entry, could soon see what manner of man he had to deal with. He was small and very plainly dressed, and the look of him, even at that distance, brought a feeling of foreboding in the watcher. Utterson made straight for Jekyll's door, crossing the roadway to save time; and as he came, he drew a key from his pocket like one approaching home.

> The author describes Mr. Hyde's breath as "hissing." What image do you think the author is trying to convey?

Mr. Utterson stepped out and touched him on the back of the shoulder as he passed. "Mr. Hyde, I presume?"

Mr. Hyde shrank back with a hissing intake of the breath. But his fear was only momentary; and though he did not look Utterson in the face, he answered coolly enough: "That is my name. What do you want?"

"I am Dr. Jekyll's lawyer, Mr. Utterson. Is Dr. Jekyll home, by chance?"

"You will not find Dr. Jekyll here," replied Mr. Hyde. Without looking up, he suddenly asked, "How did you know me?"

"I put the ball in your court," said Mr. Utterson. "Will you do me a favor?"

"With pleasure," replied the other. "What shall it be?"

"Will you let me see your face?" asked the lawyer.

Mr. Hyde appeared to hesitate, and then, as if upon some sudden reflection, turned around

Continued on the next page ➡

Continued from the previous page

with an air of defiance; and the pair stared at each other for a few seconds.

Mr. Hyde was pale and fiendish; he gave an impression of deformity without any nameable malformation, he had a displeasing smile, he had borne himself to Utterson with a sort of murderous mixture of timidity and boldness, and he spoke with a husky, whispering and somewhat broken voice; all these were points against him, but not all of these together could explain the hitherto unknown disgust, loathing, and fear with which Mr. Utterson regarded him.

> When the author states that Mr. Hyde "snarled a savage laugh," to what is he indirectly comparing Mr. Hyde?

There must be something else, thought the perplexed gentleman. *There is something more, if I could find a name for it. The man seems hardly human! O my poor old Harry Jekyll, if ever I read the devil's signature upon a face, it is on that of your new friend.*

"Now I shall recognize you," said Mr. Utterson, "in case we run into each other again."

"Yes," returned Mr. Hyde. "How did you know me?"

"We have common friends," said Mr. Utterson.

"Common friends?" echoed Mr. Hyde, a little hoarsely. "Who are they?"

> What is the overall tone of the passage?

"Dr. Jekyll, for instance," said Mr. Utterson.

Mr. Hyde snarled a savage laugh; and the next moment, with extraordinary quickness, he had unlocked the door and disappeared into the house.

Why would this passage not be considered humorous?

Apply It

Read the poem. Pay attention to how the descriptive words in each stanza affect its tone. Answer the questions that follow.

excerpted and adapted from

The Bells

by Edgar Allen Poe

I

Hear the sleighs with the bells—
Silver bells!
What a world of merriment their melody foretells!
How they tinkle, tinkle, tinkle,
5   In the icy air of night!
While the stars that oversprinkle
All the heavens seem to twinkle
With a crystalline delight;
Keeping time, time, time,
10   In a sort of ancient rhyme,
To the tintinnabulation that so musically wells
From the bells, bells, bells, bells,
Bells, bells, bells—
From the jingling and the tinkling of the bells.

II

15   Hear the mellow wedding bells—
Golden bells!
What a world of happiness their harmony foretells!
Through the balmy air of night
How they ring out their delight!
20   From the molten-golden notes,
And all in tune,
What a liquid ditty floats
To the turtle-dove that listens, while she gloats
On the moon!
25   Oh, from out the sounding cells
What a gush of euphony voluminously wells!
How it swells!
How it dwells
On the Future! How it tells

Continued on the next page ➡

Continued from the previous page

30   Of the rapture that impels
        To the swinging and the ringing
        Of the bells, bells, bells,
        Of the bells, bells, bells, bells,
        Bells, bells, bells—
35   To the rhyming and the chiming of the bells!

III

        Hear the loud alarm bells—
        Brazen bells!
        What a tale of terror, now, their turbulency tells!
        In the startled ear of night
40   How they scream out their affright!
        Too much horrified to speak,
        They can only shriek, shriek,
        Out of tune,
        In a clamorous appealing to the mercy of the fire,
45   In a mad expostulation with the deaf and frantic fire,
        Leaping higher, higher, higher,
        With a desperate desire,
        And a resolute endeavor
        Now—now to sit or never,
50   By the side of the pale-faced moon.
        Oh, the bells, bells, bells!
        What a tale their terror tells
        Of despair!
        How they clang, and clash, and roar!
55   What a horror they outpour
        On the bosom of the palpitating air!
        Yet the ear it fully knows,
        By the twanging
        And the clanging,

60   How the danger ebbs and flows;
        Yet the ear distinctly tells,
        In the jangling
        And the wrangling,
        How the danger sinks and swells,
65   By the sinking or the swelling in the anger of the bells—
        Of the bells,
        Of the bells, bells, bells, bells,
        Bells, bells, bells—
        In the clamor and the clangor of the bells!

Answer these questions about "The Bells." Write your answers in complete sentences.

1. What is the tone of the first stanza of this poem?

_____

_____

2. What words or phrases reflect the tone of the first stanza?

_____

_____

3. How does the tone shift in the third stanza of the poem?

_____

_____

4. What words or phrases reflect the tone shift of the third stanza?

_____

_____

5. In the first stanza, the bells "twinkle" and "jingle." By the third stanza, they "clang, clash, and roar." How does the *sound* of these words reflect the tone of these two stanzas?

_____

_____

Compare and Contrast Text Structures and Styles

Learn About It

An author of fiction can present his or her ideas in any of three forms—a story, a poem, or a drama. **Stories** are written in prose and are divided into sentences and paragraphs. Their structure most closely resembles spoken or written language. **Poems** are arranged in lines and stanzas and make use of various literary devices to convey a feeling or describe an abstract idea. Poems often have rhythm, meter, and rhyme. **Dramas** can be divided into acts and scenes. Dramas use dialogue and stage direction to emphasize the interaction between characters.

Read the passages. As you read, pay attention to how each text structure helps convey the author's message.

excerpted from
"My Love Is Like a Red, Red Rose"
by Robert Burns

O my Love is like a red, red rose
That's newly sprung in June;
O my Love is like the melody
That's sweetly played in tune.

At First Sight

When we first laid eyes on one another, it was like a scene in a movie: everything went into slow motion, and the figures around us fell out of focus, until all that was left was the two of us.

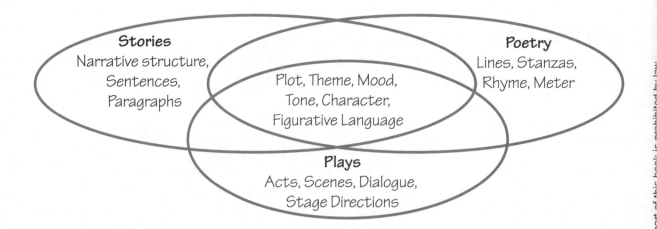

Try It

Read the passages. As you read, pay attention to how the text structure contributes to the message the author is trying to convey. Use the questions to help you.

The following poem, written in 1893, is engraved on a plaque inside the pedestal on which the Statue of Liberty stands. The Greek Colossus of Rhodes was one of the seven wonders of the ancient world.

The New Colossus
by Emma Lazarus

Not like the brazen giant of Greek fame,
With conquering limbs astride from land to land;
Here at our sea-washed, sunset gates shall stand
A mighty woman with a torch, whose flame
5   Is the imprisoned lightning, and her name
Mother of Exiles. From her beacon-hand
Glows world-wide welcome; her mild eyes command
The air-bridged harbor that twin cities frame.
"Keep, ancient lands, your storied pomp!" cries she
10   With silent lips. "Give me your tired, your poor,
Your huddled masses yearning to breathe free,
The wretched refuse of your teeming shore.
Send these, the homeless, tempest-tossed to me,
I lift my lamp beside the golden door!"

> How does the author use metaphor in this poem?

> What does the author's word choice tell you about the tone of this poem? How does she feel about her subject?

53

excerpted and adapted from

The Melting-Pot
by Israel Zangwill

Setting: The living room of MENDEL QUIXANO in New York City, circa 1909. As the scene opens, MENDEL is waiting with VERA REVENDAL, operator of a local charity, for the return of his nephew, DAVID.

DAVID is seen and heard passing the left window, still singing the national hymn; but it breaks off abruptly as he throws open the door and appears on the threshold, a buoyant figure in a cloak and a broad-brimmed hat, carrying a violin case. He is a sunny, handsome youth who speaks with a slight German accent.

DAVID: Isn't it a beautiful world, uncle? (*He closes the inner door, then perceives the visitor with amazement.*) Oh, Miss Revendal's here! (*He removes his hat and looks at her with boyish reverence and wonder.*)

VERA: (*smiling*) Don't look so surprised—I haven't fallen from heaven like the snow.

DAVID: If I had only known you were waiting….

> How does the dialogue between David and Vera help David express his feelings about America?

VERA: (*smiling*) Oh, it's no trouble, I was just telling your uncle that we would love to have you perform again at the shelter next week!

DAVID: (*smiles broadly with pleasure*) Oh, Miss Revendal! That's great!

VERA: But we can't offer you a fee.

DAVID: A fee! I'd pay a fee to see all those happy immigrants you gather together—Dutchmen and Greeks, Poles and Norwegians, Welsh and Armenians. It would be as good as going to Ellis Island.

VERA: (*smiling*) Who on Earth wants to go to Ellis Island?

DAVID: Oh, I love going to Ellis Island to watch the ships coming in from Europe, and to think that all those weary, sea-tossed wanderers are feeling what *I* felt when America first stretched out her great hand to *me*!

VERA: (*softly*) Were you very happy?

> How do the stage directions help heighten the emotion of this scene?

DAVID: It was heaven. You must remember that all my life I had heard of America—everybody in our town had friends there or was going there or got money orders from there. The earliest game I played at was selling off my toy furniture and setting up in America. All my life America was waiting, beckoning, shining—the place where God would wipe away tears from all faces.

MENDEL: (*rises*) Now, now, David, don't get excited. (*approaches him*)

DAVID: To think that the same great torch of liberty which threw its light across all the broad seas and lands into my little garret in Russia, is shining also for all those other weeping millions of Europe, shining wherever men hunger and are oppressed!

MENDEL: (*laying a hand on David's shoulder*) Now sit down and—

DAVID: Oh, Miss Revendal, when I look at our Statue of Liberty, I just seem to hear the voice of America crying: "Come unto me all ye that labor and are heavy laden and I will give you rest!" (*He is now almost sobbing.*)

MENDEL: Don't get excited—you know it is bad for you.

DAVID: But Miss Revendal asked—and I want to explain to her what America means to me.

HOTS Understand

How is Emma Lazarus able to express similar feelings about America that Israel Zangwill has in fewer words?

Apply It

Read the passages. As you read, try to identify how the elements of stories and poems are used. Answer the questions that follow.

The Marathon

The race wasn't even halfway over, and already Phillip could feel his eyes start to sting from the sweat pouring down his brow. As he wiped his face with the front of his shirt, he chided himself for not wearing a headband, as his mother had told him to do. (She would, he was certain, remind him of that later.) Phillip convinced himself that it would have looked silly, and he didn't want yet another thing making him feel self-conscious. He was getting enough stares from strangers as it was.

The giddiness that had followed the starting gun seemed like a distant memory, and the finish line ahead like some child's dream. The runners, who had been bunched like sweat socks at the starting gate, were now spaced out into their separate orbits, each left to his own thoughts and his own private pains. Several runners had already succumbed to cramps or sore ankles, or just plain exhaustion. Phillip's lungs heaved like a huge set of bellows beneath his chest—he was going to have to do a better job of regulating his breathing if he was going to last. There was a time when he wouldn't even have to think about that sort of thing, but running didn't come as easy as it did in the days before the accident. Then again, few things did.

Phillip could remember the way his arms and shoulders used to tense up and ache as he supported himself on the parallel bars during those grueling early therapy sessions. Back then, getting to the other side of the room seemed like a marathon in and of itself. He began to relax a bit as he realized how freely his arms swung now as he ran, keeping time with the rhythmic thumping of his prosthetic legs.

As the race wore on, Phillip's attention continued to turn inward—he found that the more he focused on what he was thinking, the less he would realize how much his body was starting to ache. What was it that had allowed him to sustain himself during those dark times? It certainly wasn't simple optimism—that had never really been his strong suit. Maybe it was just plain old stubbornness. Phillip had always been the type of person who would run when he was told to walk, so when the doctors told him he would never walk again, it seemed perfectly natural for him to say, "Fine. I guess I'll just run, then."

Phillip was pulled out of his reverie by—what was that sound? Cheering! He was almost there. Pain was no longer an issue; he even thought he felt his artificial limbs grow stronger as he came down the home stretch. He wasn't going to win, but winning wasn't really the point. He had come a long way, and that's all that really mattered.

Invictus

by William Ernest Henley

Out of the night that covers me,
Black as the Pit from pole to pole,
I thank whatever gods may be
For my unconquerable soul.

5   In the fell clutch of circumstance
I have not winced nor cried aloud.
Under the bludgeonings of chance
My head is bloody, but unbowed.

Beyond this place of wrath and tears
10   Looms but the Horror of the shade,
And yet the menace of the years
Finds, and shall find, me unafraid.

It matters not how strait the gate,
How charged with punishments the scroll.
15   I am the master of my fate:
I am the captain of my soul.

Answer these questions about "The Marathon" and "Invictus." Write your answers in complete sentences.

1. What themes do "The Marathon" and "Invictus" have in common?

_____

_____

2. How does the text structure of "The Marathon" allow its author to heighten the suspense of the story?

_____

_____

3. How does the tone of "The Marathon" differ from that of "Invictus"?

_____

_____

4. How does the text structure of "The Marathon" allow the reader to develop a more personal relationship with the narrative of the story?

_____

_____

5. "The Marathon" has five long paragraphs. "Invictus" has only four short stanzas, yet both passages convey a similar message. What elements of poetry allow the author of "Invictus" to express so much in just a few words?

_____

_____

Analyze Modern Fiction and Myths

Learn About It

Ancient cultures relied on traditional stories called **myths** to make sense of the world around them. These myths use gods and goddesses, magic, or the supernatural to explain natural events, to teach history, and to provide models of how people should behave. All cultures have their own myths, but the myths of ancient Greece and Rome have had the greatest influence on Western literature. For centuries, authors have alluded to Greek and Roman characters and stories in their writing. Even today, many movies and television shows make references to ancient Greek and Roman myths.

Read the passage. As you read, pay attention to the elements that make this passage a myth.

Arachne was the greatest weaver in the world. She boasted that her work was even better than that of the gods. Minerva, the goddess of wisdom, heard this and challenged her to a weaving contest. Minerva barely won, and taunted Arachne mercilessly. When Arachne died, Minerva regretted her behavior, and brought Arachne back to life as a spider. This explains why spiders weave such beautiful webs.

Elements of Myths	Elements of Modern Fiction
Characters include gods or heroes	Characters may be realistic or imaginary
Make use of magic or the supernatural	Events may be realistic or imaginary
Explain how something works or was created	Focuses on the lives of the characters
Teach lessons about proper human behavior	May or may not teach a lesson about human behavior

Try It

Read the passages. As you read, try to identify how elements of myths are used in each passage. Use the questions to help you.

Echo and Narcissus

Hera, the queen of the gods, was known for her unmatched jealousy. So when she believed that a young goddess named Echo had fallen in love with her husband Zeus, Hera decided to punish her. She took away Echo's ability to speak her own thoughts; from then on, Echo could only repeat what others said to her.

> What natural events does this myth explain?

In fact, Echo had fallen in love with a mortal named Narcissus. Narcissus was famous not only for his great beauty, but also for the scorn and ridicule with which he treated the unlucky women who fell in love with him. Echo tried to express her feelings for him, but as a result of Hera's curse, she could only repeat the cruel things Narcissus said to her. Despairing, she retreated to lonely places in caves and mountains, where her voice can still be heard today.

> What is Narcissus's main character trait? What lesson does this story teach about that character trait?

Nemesis, the goddess of revenge, decided to punish Narcissus for his arrogance. One day, she lured Narcissus to a pool of water. When he bent over the pool to get a drink, he saw his own reflection, and fell hopelessly in love with himself. Narcissus then knew his lovers' pain: he could never reach the reflection he saw in the water, but was so entranced that he could not pull himself away. He stayed in that very spot admiring himself, until he wasted away and died. On the spot where he lay grew a new and beautiful flower, which bears Narcissus's name to this day.

excerpted and adapted from

The Picture of Dorian Gray
by Oscar Wilde

Within his circle of young noblemen, Dorian Gray was considered by far the most handsome. Inspired by his striking appearance, a world-renowned artist painted Dorian's portrait, and all agreed that the resulting painting bore an amazing resemblance to its subject. Taken by the flattery of his admirers, and influenced by his reckless friends, Dorian became convinced that beauty and pleasure were the only things that mattered in life. At the same time, he was saddened by the thought that his beauty would fade away as he grew older. Dorian jokingly offered to sell his soul in exchange for the gift of eternal youth and beauty. To his surprise, his wish was granted, in the form of the mysterious portrait.

After coldly breaking the heart of a young actress named Sybil, Dorian noticed that his picture had somehow grown uglier. He discovered that while the painting changed to reflect his wickedness and age, he himself remained young and beautiful. Dorian devoted the rest of his life to evil and vanity; he did not age a day, but the figure in the painting grew old and disfigured to reflect his sins. After eighteen years of living immorally, Dorian was desperate to save his soul and tried to destroy the painting with a knife. His servants heard a cry from the room where the portrait was hung, and were shocked to find Dorian's withered and wrinkled body lying beneath the mysterious portrait, which now looked just as it had the day it was painted.

> How is Dorian Gray similar to Narcissus? How do they treat the other characters in their stories?

> How is the supernatural represented in this story?

HOTS Analyze

How does "The Picture of Dorian Gray" draw on elements from the story of Narcissus?

Apply It

Read the passages. As you read, try to identify how elements of myths are used in each passage. Answer the questions that follow.

The Myth of Prometheus

At the dawn of history, Prometheus was considered the wisest of the gods. He belonged to the race of Titans that ruled the universe before Zeus and his siblings rose to overthrow them. Prometheus aided Zeus in his revolt, and as a reward for his assistance, Zeus allowed Prometheus to remain at his new palace at Olympus, and charged him with the task of creating living beings to inhabit the newly created Earth.

Prometheus, whose name means "forethought," was aided in his work by his brother Epimetheus, whose name means "afterthought." While Prometheus carefully shaped the new creatures out of clay, Epimetheus assigned certain advantages to each creature to help it survive in the harsh wilderness. This is how birds came to have wings, bears came to have great size and strength, and lions came to have sharp teeth and claws. But Epimetheus planned poorly, so that when it was time to create human beings, he had already given all of nature's gifts to the other creatures. To make up for his brother's error, Prometheus made human beings stand tall and upright, in the image of the gods. He endowed them with the divine spark of intelligence, and taught them all of the civilized arts, including mathematics, agriculture, architecture, and writing. Humans did not have the ability to see the future as the gods did, so Prometheus gave them the gift of hope instead.

Zeus disliked these human beings, but had no power to destroy what another immortal had made. Instead, he denied humans immortality, and confined them to Earth, where they were still vulnerable to the wild creatures and harsh elements. Prometheus pitied humankind, so he stole the sacred fire from Zeus's palace at Olympus and passed it along to humans. With this fire, they could protect themselves from predators, warm themselves in the cold, and guide themselves by its light in the darkness. Without this gift, there could be no civilization.

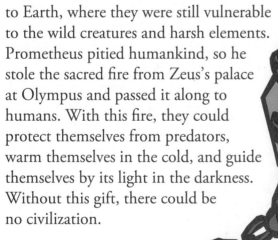

Continued on the next page ➤

Continued from the previous page

Zeus was furious at Prometheus's treachery and the theft of the sacred fire. He ordered his two servants, Force and Violence, to seize Prometheus and have him chained to a large rock in a barren mountain range, where he was perpetually tormented by a giant eagle. Each day, the eagle would tear at Prometheus's liver. Though immortal, Prometheus could still feel pain, and during the night his liver would regenerate, so his torments would begin anew the next day. Years later, the hero Hercules killed the eagle with his arrows and freed Prometheus from his chains. For centuries afterward, humans sacrificed animal livers to the gods in honor of Prometheus, whom they regarded as the savior of humankind.

excerpted and adapted from

Frankenstein, or the Modern Prometheus
by Mary Shelley

After days and nights of incredible labor and fatigue, I succeeded in discovering the cause of generation and life; nay, more, I became myself capable of bestowing animation upon lifeless matter!

The astonishment that I had at first experienced on this discovery soon gave place to delight and rapture. What had been the study and desire of the wisest men since the creation of the world was now within my grasp. I was like the one who had been buried with the dead, and found a passage to life.

I see by your eagerness, and the wonder and hope which your eyes express, that you expect to be informed of the secret with which I am acquainted; that cannot be: listen patiently until the end of my story, and you will easily perceive why I am reserved upon that subject. Learn from me, if not by my warnings, at least by my example, how catastrophic it is to meddle with the forces of creation. How dangerous is the acquirement of knowledge, and how much happier that man is who believes his native town to be the world, than he who aspires to become greater than his nature will allow!

It was on a dreary night of November that I beheld the accomplishment of all of my work. With an anxiety that almost amounted to agony, I collected the instruments of life around me, so that I might infuse a spark of being into the lifeless corpse that lay on the operating table in my laboratory. It was already one in the morning, and my candle was nearly burnt out, when, by the glimmer of the half-extinguished light, I saw the dull yellow eye of the creature open; it breathed hard, and a convulsive motion agitated its limbs.

Continued on the next page ➡

Continued from the previous page

How can I describe my emotions at this catastrophe, or how to describe the wretched being I had created? His limbs were in proportion, and I had selected his features as beautiful. Beautiful! Good heavens! No mortal could support the horror of that face. A mummy given life again could not be so hideous as that wretch. I had gazed on him while unfinished, and he was ugly then; but when those muscles and joints were rendered capable of motion, it became a thing such as even the devil could not have conceived. His yellow skin scarcely covered the work of muscles and arteries beneath; his hair was of a lustrous black, and flowing; his teeth of a pearly whiteness; but these luxuries only formed a more horrid contrast with his watery eyes, which seemed almost of the same color as his shriveled complexion and straight black lips.

I had worked hard for nearly two years, for the sole purpose of infusing life into an inanimate body. For this I had deprived myself of rest and health. I had desired it with an ardor that far exceeded moderation; but now that I had finished, the beauty of the dream vanished, and breathless horror and disgust filled my heart.

Answer these questions about "The Myth of Prometheus" and "Frankenstein." Write your answers in complete sentences.

1. What natural events does "The Myth of Prometheus" explain?

_____

_____

2. Mary Shelley, the author of "Frankenstein," gave it an alternate title: "The Modern Prometheus." How is the narrator of "Frankenstein" like Prometheus?

_____

_____

3. How does the narrator of "Frankenstein" react to his creation?

_____

_____

4. How is Prometheus's reaction to human beings different than Frankenstein's reaction to his creation?

_____

_____

5. Prometheus uses his divine powers to mold human beings. What "magic" does the narrator of "Frankenstein" use to create life?

_____

_____

6. Judging from the tone and the outcome of the story, how do you think the author of "Frankenstein" might feel about this kind of "magic"?

_____

_____

Analyze Modern Fiction and Traditional Stories

Learn About It

Traditional stories and **folktales** are similar to myths in that they are passed down from generation to generation. Like myths, folktales often incorporate magic or the supernatural. But while myths include gods or heroes, the main characters of folktales are mostly humans, or objects or animals that act like humans. Folktales will often make use of exaggeration to make their messages clearer or more humorous. Their purpose is not only to entertain, but also to define and reinforce cultural values. Folktales warn against the dangers of greed, vanity, and envy, and stress the benefits of hard work, good judgment, and kindness.

Read the passage. As you read, pay attention to what makes this passage a folktale.

The Wind and the Sun
by Aesop

One day, Wind and Sun were arguing about who was stronger. A traveler approached, and they agreed that whoever could remove his cloak first was the stronger. Wind tried to blow the man's cloak away, but this only made the traveler tighten it further. Sun shined warmly, and the man took his cloak off. This shows that kindness is sometimes more effective than force.

Elements of a Folktale	Elements of Modern Fiction
Characters that are people, objects, or animals	Characters are usually people
An element of magic or the supernatural	May or may not include magic
Defines and reinforces cultural values	May or may not reinforce cultural values

Try It

Read the passages. As you read, pay attention to how elements of folktales are used to promote cultural values. Use the questions to help you.

The Legend of John Henry

John Henry was the mightiest man to ever work the Chesapeake and Ohio Railroad. At over six feet tall and 200 pounds, John was a giant for his day. He started working for the railroad right around the time the tracks hit Big Bend Mountain. The bosses decided it would be too expensive to build around the mountain, so they decided to drill a tunnel right through it. It was grueling work, but no one could split rock like big John. He swung a huge fourteen-pound hammer, and drilled faster and farther than anyone.

> **What cultural values does the legend of John Henry promote?**

One day, an inventor came to Big Bend with a newfangled creation: a steam-powered drill, one that he said could do the work of scores of men.

"Well, it ain't faster than ol' John here," said the foreman. "I'll betcha a hundred dollars that John'll leave that thing in the dust."

> **What is the supernatural element of this folktale?**

The inventor took the bet, and John picked up not one but two twenty-pound hammers and went to work. A cloud of rubble rose as John swung his hammers feverishly, one in each hand. After a half hour, John had drilled through over fourteen feet of rock, while the mechanical drill managed only nine. The men whooped and cheered, not noticing that John had collapsed. The exertion was more than even his mighty heart could stand, and he fell to the ground and died. To this day, some say that if you pass by Big Bend, you can still hear the sound of John's hammers splitting that rock.

69

Checkmate

I'll admit it: Steve was the smartest guy I'd ever met. But there was a laziness to his intelligence that made it hard to take him seriously. He had aced his placement tests, but that seemed to be more the result of simple dumb luck than any sort of studiousness. He never seemed stressed, and no one ever saw him study, even during exams time.

That's why I was amused when I heard that Steve had taken up Raj's challenge. Nothing was lazy about Raj, and everyone knew that the chess program he had written was unbeatable. The best Ivan had been able to do against it was two losses and four draws, and he was some sort of chess champion back in Russia. The fact that Steve would even step to the challenge seemed like a joke.

Raj was already in a triumphant mood when Steve showed up for the match. Steve, for his part, looked like he had just woken up. So you can imagine how surprised we all were when Steve beat the computer four matches in a row. Just like that. When it was all over, Raj looked like someone had punched him in the stomach.

I cornered Steve after the match. "How did you do that?" I asked.

"Simple. I reasoned that the only way to beat the computer was to level the playing field, so I just hacked into Raj's program and rewrote it."

Like I said, Steve was the smartest guy I'd ever met.

> Which element of folktales is missing from the second story?

> How is the portrayal of technology in this story different from the portrayal of technology in "The Legend of John Henry"?

How does "Checkmate" draw on elements from "The Legend of John Henry"?

Apply It

Read the passages. As you read, try to identify the elements of folktales in the stories. Answer the questions that follow.

adapted from

The Wolf and the Fox

by The Brothers Grimm

The wolf and the fox were constant companions as they traveled through the forest together, but they were not exactly friends. Whatever the wolf wished, the fox was compelled to do, for he was the weaker of the two. Once, as they were walking through the forest, the wolf said, "Fox, get me something to eat, or I will eat you instead."

The fox answered, "I know a farmhouse where the wife is baking pancakes tonight; we can get some for ourselves."

They went to the farmhouse, and the fox sneaked into the kitchen and found a plate on which there was a stack of pancakes. Making sure no one was watching, he stole six of them, which he carried out to the wolf. The wolf swallowed down the pancakes in an instant, and said, "They make me want more!"

The wolf burst into the kitchen himself, and tore the whole plate down so that it broke in pieces. This made such a great noise that the wife came out, and when she saw the wolf she beat him with a broom, chasing him out into the forest.

"You misled me!" cried the wolf. "The wife caught me and beat me with her broom."

But the fox replied, "Well, it wouldn't have happened it you weren't such a glutton."

The next day, when they were out together, and the wolf could only limp along painfully, he said, "Fox, get me something to eat, or I will eat you instead."

The fox answered, "I know a man who has some salted meat in his cellar; we will get that."

Said the wolf, "I'll go with you this time, so you can help me escape if we get caught."

Continued on the next page ➤

Continued from the previous page

When the pair reached the man's cellar through a hole they had dug, they found huge barrels filled with meat. The wolf attacked them instantly and cried, "There is plenty of time to eat all of this meat!" The fox liked it also, but kept his eyes on the stairs that led up to the man's kitchen, and often ran to the hole by which they had come in, to make sure he was still thin enough to slip through it. The wolf said, "Why do you look so nervous, and why do you keep running in and out?"

"I must see that no one is coming," replied the fox. "Don't eat too much!"

Then said the wolf, "I won't leave until every barrel is empty." Soon the farmer, who had heard noise coming from his cellar, came down the stairs. When the fox saw him coming, he jumped out of the hole in one bounce. The wolf wanted to follow him, but he had made himself so fat with eating that he could not fit through the hole. The wolf howled as the farmer beat his backside with a stick, but the fox bounded into the forest, glad to be free of his old gluttonous master.

excerpted and adapted from

How Much Land Does a Man Need?
by Leo Tolstoy

Once there was an old peasant named Pahom who, in repayment for a debt to a large landowner, was allowed to take as much of the landowner's land as he could walk in a day. The landowner made one condition: Pahom had to start walking at sunrise, and return to the spot at which he started by sunset, or else he would forfeit everything he had earned that day.

On the appointed day, Pahom woke up well before sunrise to prepare himself. When he arrived at the landowner's estate, the landowner threw his cap upon the ground and said:

"This will be the mark. Start from here, and return here again. All the land you go round shall be yours."

Once the sun had peeked over the horizon, Pahom set out on his way. When the sun was fully risen, Pahom looked back. At a rough guess he concluded that he had walked three miles. After he completed one side of his journey, Pahom began to grow tired: he looked at the sun and saw that it was noon. After sitting a little while, he went on again, but it had become terribly hot, and he felt sleepy.

"Ah!" thought Pahom, "I have made the sides too long; I must make this one shorter." And he went along the third side, stepping faster. After he completed this side, Pahom went straight toward the landowner's house, but he now walked with difficulty. He was exhausted with the heat, and his legs began to fail. He longed to rest, but he was desperate to get back before sunset.

"What shall I do?" he thought again. "I have grasped too much, and ruined the whole affair! I can't get there before the sun sets."

And this fear made him still more breathless. Pahom went on running; his heart was beating like a hammer, and his legs were giving way as if they did not belong to him. Though afraid of death, he could not stop. "After having run all that way they will call me a fool if I stop now," thought he.

Continued on the next page ➤

Continued from the previous page

Pahom looked at the sun, which had reached the horizon: one side of it had already disappeared. With all his remaining strength he rushed on, bending his body forward so that his legs could hardly follow fast enough to keep him from falling. At last, he reached the landowner's house, but his legs gave way beneath him, and he fell forward and reached the cap with his hands.

"Ah, what a fine fellow!" exclaimed the landowner. "He has gained much land!"

But it was all for nothing, for the old peasant had extended himself beyond the point of exhaustion. Poor Pahom was dead!

Answer these questions about "The Wolf and the Fox" and "How Much Land Does a Man Need?" Write your answers in complete sentences.

1. What cultural values does "The Wolf and the Fox" promote?

_____

_____

2. How are the cultural values of "The Wolf and the Fox" reflected in "How Much Land Does a Man Need?"?

_____

_____

3. What is an example of exaggeration in "The Wolf and the Fox"?

_____

_____

4. How does this exaggeration make the tone of "The Wolf and the Fox" different from "How Much Land Does a Man Need?"?

_____

_____

Graphic Organizers

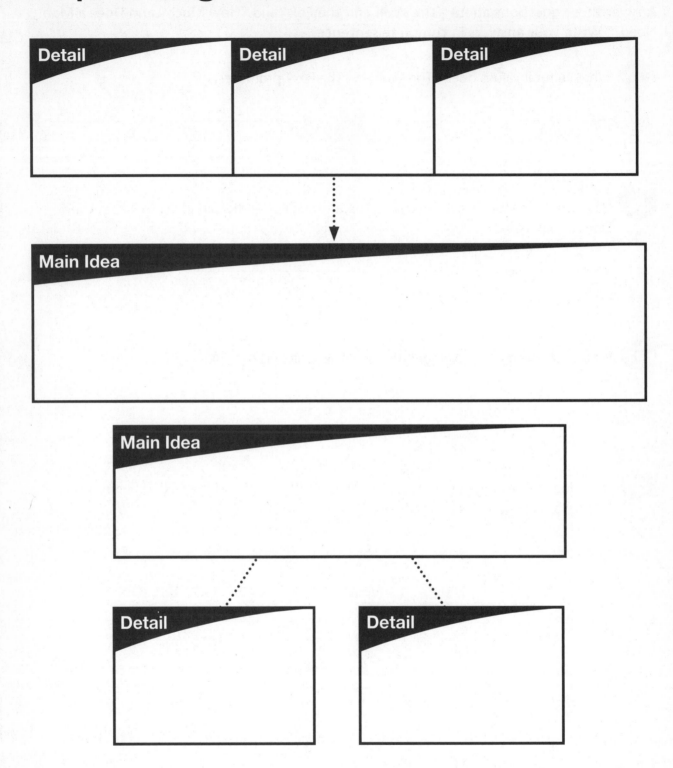

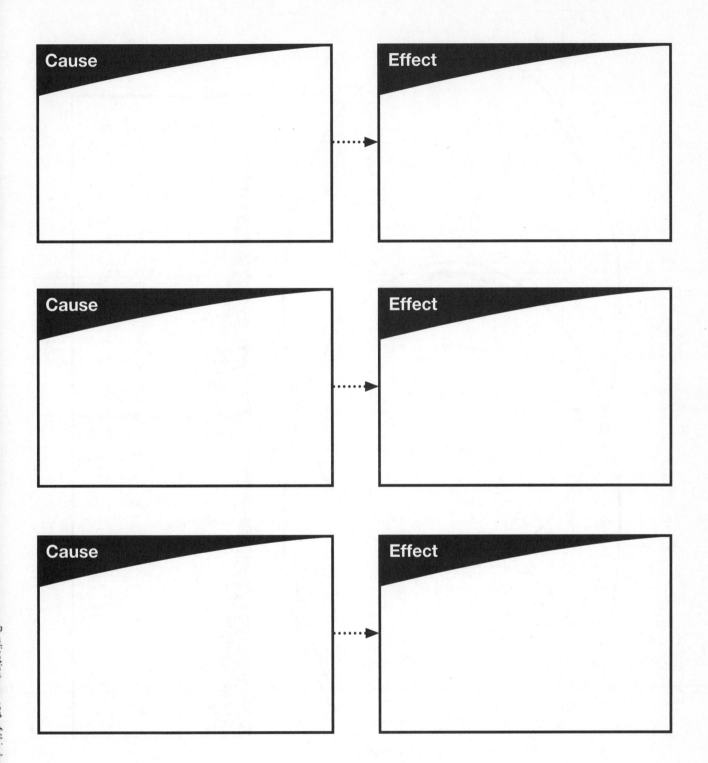

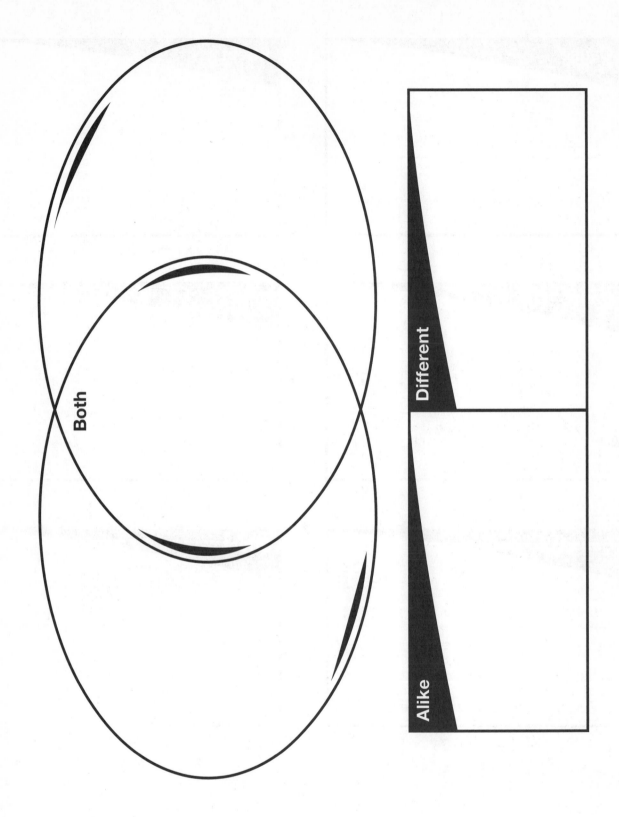

Both

Different

Alike

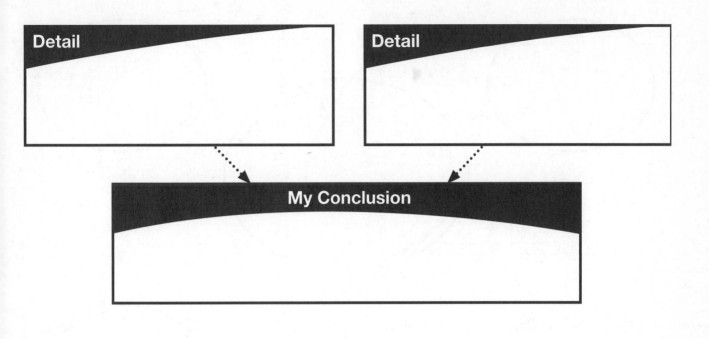

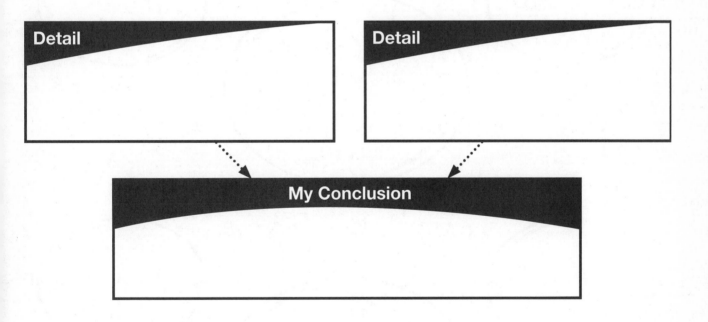

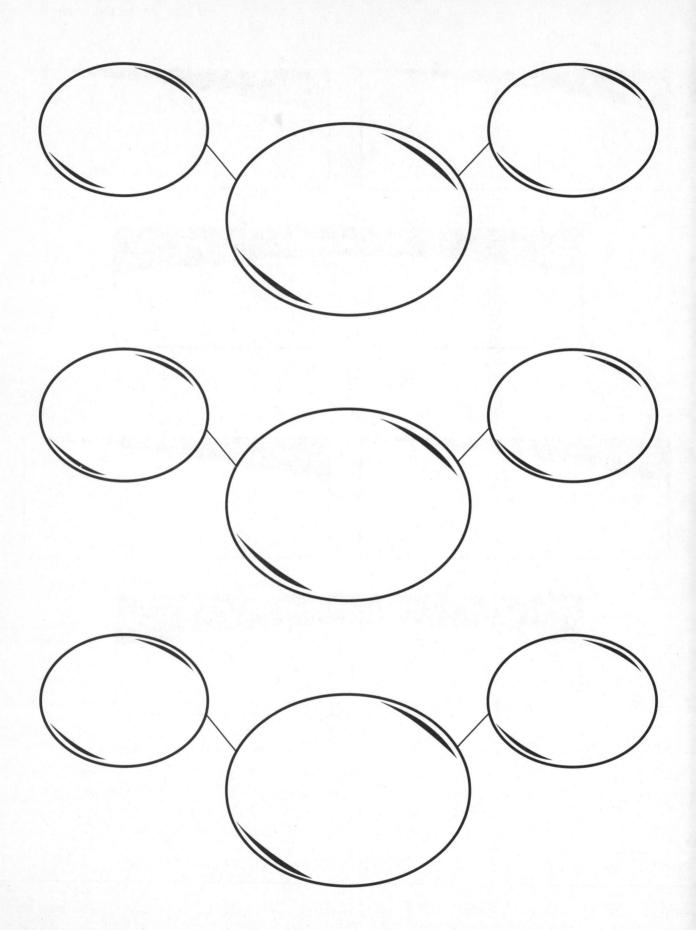